UNSTOPPABLE

MONISHA THOMAS

INDIA • SINGAPORE • MALAYSIA

To all chasing dreams,
Knitting stories
Inked in love.

Contents

Foreword

The heart always has a little more room, just when you think it doesn't have anymore. Sometimes we empty it out when it has filled to overflowing, making room for more.

Monisha Thomas (née Mathews) has done just that, as she has filled the pages with poetically arranged words. She has made herself vulnerable in sharing with the world her deep thoughts that were kept hidden, through these 5o-odd poems.

It is my honour to read the poems from the thoughts of a little school girl I once knew, to the lines of a mature, graceful woman she has now become. It is refreshing to see how she has retained her grace and poise over the decades, untarnished by cynicism or skepticism.

Manna Abraham

Author of Heart of the Circus

Acknowledgements

If my work can spark a conversation, or comfort anyone looking up for encouragement, hope and affirmation, then I am fulfilling in part, the reason this book has been published.

That said, poetry is like a crocheted blanket painstakingly woven in love to help you snuggle up and get past a harsh wintry night. Whatever be the season in your life, I hope this little book may add a dollop of colour and add fresh perspective to relatable situations in life.

Everyone thrives in an oasis. My work would have been a shrivelled piece sans the help pouring in to complete it. Encouragement of friends and family pushed me to get down to publishing my first collection of poetry.

Manu believed in me always and egged me on,

Michelle tugged at my heartstrings every time I wrote something for her.

Marie hooted for me to get going and not to shy away from putting my work out there,

My mom always believed I have some more to offer and I delight in giving her my best,

Thank you for making me unstoppable!

JOY

Summer Soirée

My heart's in a flutter-

Surely there's something

In the air that tickles my senses,

And wakes up the inner child

In me,

to savor sunny days

and endless blue skies!

The rushing winds and deafening roar,

Of the azure ocean

Tempts me to trip

Down the cobbled path

leading me gently to

The edge of turbulent blue waters...

To dip my feet in that frothy sea

Hugging the shores sparingly!

That tug of the swirling waves

beckons me to feel carefree

And splash around a bit,

To the rhythm of the thumping sea
A thousand drums in unison that
Makes my heart almost skip a beat!

'Neath the speckled skies above
A canopy of divine blue
I lightly tread upon the silky sand,
With a spring in my step.
My senses are drenched
And soaked,
In that indulgent moment
Heady with hints of
tropical scents
Seeping through the seams
Of my soul!
Prepped and ready
To spread my wings
Beyond the blues
And swoop yet again
To join a summer soirée of sorts
To celebrate the creative
magic of summertime!
There is a distinct roar

that rises

From the depth of my soul,

that is ripe to harvest

And thresh some

unbridled fun under the sun!

The resplendent sky shimmers

And clothes me in her amber glow

Only to melt in a moment

to reveal

Glorious purple tassels

of the satin royal robes

Of my King who rules the skies.

Theatrics in the Skies

Through the frosted glass
I gape in wonder
As I see glistening clouds
That look like torched meringue peaks
On a fluffy scrumptious cake!
Holding my breath
I sat mesmerized in awe
Cruising over that
majestic sea of clouds!
It's certainly a privilege
To hit a sea state of absolute calm
Somewhere at 35000 feet!

Suddenly out of the blue
Caught unawares
I frantically held on the seat
White knuckled my colour drained

As the plane just nose dived
Hurtling through a turbulent patch
through mounds of spooky grey
For the longest five minutes
Of my life!
The theatrics in the skies
calmed down for a bit
Until the drama peaked yet again
with the pesky sun
Just doing its own thing
Like a giant flashlight
Sweeps the horizon
one last time searching
For lost mariners out at sea.
The setting sun drapes the horizon
In a mystical melange of purples
And peach
With a tangerine afterglow
And an imaginary drumroll,
And slips out quietly
for the umpteenth time,
For the constellations of stars
Out there, to take

The center stage again!
Smudging the skyline
As she went
With a riot of colors
amber, gold, and pink
The sun took a bow as she plunged,
into inky darkness for a night,
To a rousing applause
Of a million twinkling stars

A sensorial feast
For the awed traveler,
Treading in awe
Strapped in an airplane,
A Witness to the Greatest Show
Happening in the troposphere!

Skipper

When the wind roared
Whipping her back,
Cracking through the bow,
And decks and the beams;
She braced and stood still.

From the rising of the sun,
Till it's setting down,
Oh! the skipper has his eyes,
Set on his Love!

The sea churned,
and frothed at her mouth,
And the winds tossed the boat,
And flung her around.

In the fiercest of storms,

He steered the battleship,

Braving roaring winds,

Riding glistening waves,

Into the setting sun.

The Story of an Oyster

Roving eyes
And hungry hearts,
Greedily scoured ocean floors,
For treasures untold.
And then one day,
A curious hustler with
An untrained eye,
Chanced upon
This oyster -
A gritty beginning
To say the least is
The story of this oysters life!
What good can come out
Of an oyster, a mollusc
Or a clam you may ask!
He prised it open and
Was astonished to find

Hidden from prying eyes -
An iridescent jewel!

The oyster, weathered many a storm
That settled in her eye
But she tucked and buried it,
Deep within,
Where it transformed
Into the toughest pearl
That stood the test of time.

When the curious harvester
Snapped the mantle
Up in two,
In the hollow of his palm;
He let out a muffled gasp
As he held the precious pearl
Gently in his hand.
He stared reverently
At this priceless jewel
Swathed in a lustrous glow!

This oyster was happy just the same
On the ocean bed my friend,
Until it was time
To reveal,
The glorious mother pearl
Signs of a weathered soul.

Spangles of Gold

I hurried excitedly to watch

The rising sun one day,

When the streets were quiet

And the cloudy skies over Beppu

Seemed reluctant to reveal,

The blushing bride just yet!

I caught my breath in awe

And waited gingerly,

Scanning the horizon,

For the drama to unfold.

She demurely emerged,

creasing the skyline

With saffron

and spangles of gold,

Spilling over the taut tangerine sky,

Casting a magical spell,

Upon the shimmering waters,

Smooth as satin.

Priceless was that golden hour,
When the sandy sea shore and I
Were aglow like fireflies
Dusted in spangles of gold.
Eternally grateful, I walked away,
My heart so full, brimming with love,
And a glimmer of hope and faith,
Soaked in Light,I walked away
From the serene seaside
In the Land of the Rising Sun.

My Brainless Heart

My brainless heart,

Thumps a million times,

Forever without a break,

Never stopping for a lifetime!

Pumping rivers of ruby red

And endless love for days on end,

To the farthest corner of my soul!

Thumping to a rhythmic beat,

When life just spins

Out of control,

My dear heart

Huffs and races

To keep up

In matchless grace,

Faithfully,

Never securing for the night...

Never pausing for a break,

Watchful and alert,

My heart pumps, effortlessly.

God planted in me, a brainless heart

That loves unconditionally,

A reminder of Him

A piece of His entwined in mine.

Like a Dandelion

Once again it's time

To move

To bid adieu to my

warm and cozy home

And build again

in another port

Where the wind

blows me to.

I find myself wedged in

A moment of time when

I needed to fold up

Dreams and goals

Along with my linen and

Cartloads of clothes.

Herbs and flowers
Potted with love
Bobbed gently in the breeze
Rooting for me
Seem to plead
"Please don't go…"
It just makes me wince
to let them go.

Bruised but not broken
I am once again
swept off my feet
Like a wispy dandelion
Yet again to another port
Where I begin
All over again!

Purple Up!

On the steep slopes,
Of mountains grand,
Across the valleys,
Dotting the wild,
They often grow in abandon.
By the sidewalks and
By-lanes of life.
Dandelions.
They sway,
Bobbing and dancing across,
The windswept plains and pastures,
Surviving the rains, harsh terrains,
Whistling winds and gusty days,
Bellowing thunder and acid rains!
Some kids have faced it all
And been blown away
Only to start all over again.
Over the mountains and over the hills

Lining the sidewalks
And by-lanes again.
Thriving in rain, wind and sunshine,
They are the children of military fame!
Their dad serves the nation
Posted in the army or
May be moms in the navy
And at times flying a plane.

Often uprooted and replanted
They bloom anywhere -
By the sea or at an airbase,
Transiting homes time and again,
They are resilient and brave.
So I wear the badge
With honour and pride
Purple is the color
of my Dandelion child!

The Wall

I stare at all the photographs,

Framed and lined up on the wall,

With frayed corners,

And tell-tale smudges,

From fingertips

That held it, long enough.

I touch the glass

That's gathered dust

And gently run my fingers, Over it,

So I do not disturb,

The vivid moment

before me-

Reviving a sublime moment,

Now frozen in time.

Every frame nailed to this wall

Tells a story so vivid and is ablaze

With love and fiery emotions that

Makes my heart skip a beat.

I hold my breath

once again as

The stone rolled back,

bringing back heady moments,

that were the elixir of life.

*And now these three remain Faith, Hope, and Love.
But the greatest of these is Love.*

LOVE

You and Me

I soak up the long loving stares

The twinkle in your deep brown eyes.

I smile, for the sparkle I see

Is resonant

Of the love that binds

You and me eternally!

Days with you

Are a song and dance,

And if the music fades,

Or the sun doesn't shine,

And if you walk away

Or heaven calls me home

I know for sure

That the light we cupped

Was a magical find!

And together we have

Magnified love,

Walked on thorny ground,

On starry nights,

Nimbly

For all the world

And our children to see

An incandescent love.

Sunset Years

I will walk into
my sunset years with you
with thinning hair that's silver,
with wrinkles, and crow feet,
and a sparkling smile,
with few teeth with fancy filling,
(i got at a dentists' for quite a hefty fee.)
My creaky joints might make me slow
to keep up with the kids,
But gaunt or fat,
I hope to woo you with my smile
and giggle over stories,
Infamous ones that warm our hearts
every time it's told!
Together we will raise a toast
to all that makes us whole!

Good Father

Heroes aren't born overnight
Nor are they born with capes!
Imperfect and often hardened
By struggles of different kinds;
With squashed dreams and frayed nerves,
He suffered cuts and scrapes
caught in the barbs of life often
Growing up in difficult times,
Tricked and trapped
In subtle ways
Wronged and duped multiple times.

The pulp of human frailties
Fills his beating heart
Hemmed in by obstacles,
and trenches in his path.
He strains with all his might
Not to tilt the cart he has to push,

And stays up several nights
Standing in the gap,
with his rugged hands
he yanks his kids in the nick of time
and holds them to his chest
when he senses they are frayed
like a rag doll.
He will always be my hero
He doesn't wear a cape.

Momsie Pie

I tiptoed into
Your life
Just like that,
sauntering in
When you least expected
A baby's shrill cry,
Disrupting your calm life!
I changed you
And charged you to be
the fierce mom that you are
Ever since that special day!

And you swept me up,
Snuggled me close-
Whispering sweet nothings
Into my baby ears,
Tenderly holding me

And teaching me,
All those days;
Only to release me in time
To fly.

Stitch by stitch,
You wove into me,
Patterns that altered
And tailored my destiny.
The star- studded sky
Pales in your love,
Focused on teaching
Me constantly
To walk in grace.
And then
you let me go,
Far from your loving gaze
As I tiptoed away into
My adult life.

Oh how strange
Is the circle of life,
Where I find myself

Nursing my babies

fussing over them,

only to see them go,

tiptoe away just like me.

I hold on to love and scars,

And remember with moist eyes,

You taught me to be a mom

to give all that I have

just like you did, when I tiptoed

into your life momsiepie!

Doxie Tails

His first yelp,

whelped her heart.

She heard him,

And time stood still;

Yuki she whispered

And he was found.

Tattooed on to her heart

Forever -

A whiny weiner

Black n tan

Starved of love

Snuggled into her arms.

A saga of incredible love

Had just begun.

Taking turns to

Feed and clean

Fuss and train

A confused pup

Learned to love

All over again.

Like a zombie

she staggered through

Sleepless nights

Cleaning pee and poo

Till he grew

And got to know

His p's and q's!

The day he learned

to sit and stay

And shake a paw

Blotted out the pain

Of learning to

Be patient all over again!

Before she knew

he had her heart

And pawing hard for

All her love!

It sure has been quite a ride

Rock n roll and roll over again!

When trouble brewed

And the most desperate

Shadows loomed in

Threatening to snuff out the

Joy he brings…

Sheer love

And mustered faith

as small as

A Mustard seed

Is all that took to

See him scamper back to life!

A living miracle

A story of gritty resilience

Love and licks and loudest of all

This nasty "boii"

As she calls him

Has weathered much

And is tattooed on her heart.

Michelle

Clutching her ragged lil doll
She stood
Often beside me while I worked,
Making lunch or cleaning home!
Twirling her soft brown hair,
Big melting eyes searching mine
She would pose that question
"Mommy do you love me"
For the one hundredth time!

I bend down and draw her
Close to my heart
I soak in her scents
Of Honeysuckle or lavender
Baby shampoos and talc
I tickle her toes and hug her tight
And whisper again as always
What she needs to hear

Of how much I love her
And she gurgles in delight
"Again mamma
"Will you say that again!"

Warrior Princess

Her bouncy curls
Cascade like rivulets
That time tried so hard
to tame.
She boldly marches on
A blazing streak
Defying stifling norms of this world.
On torrid days
Her unruly mop of curly locks
Tousled by the wind,
Is an anthem that wells up
from within her.
She carries
The scent of burning embers
From the furiously fought battles
On the nights before.
She now nimbly crosses

hurdles in her path,

As she stretches and splays her limbs

And tired toes to tear through

The finishing line

with a twinkle in her eye!

Blessed be my warrior queen

Though darkness lurks around you

The light within

Wrapped in uncanny candor

Spells hope

even on pitch dark nights-

shining like a beacon

A confident heart thumping

Sending ripples of love

To the farthest shores.

Ripples of Laughter

I awkwardly walked into
That airy room full of light
booming with the voices
of my childhood friends,
I was eager to meet
After so many years!
Squeals of laughter and banter
And familiar voices
Floated in like a gentle feather,
That settled in
My outstretched palm!

My beaming friends,
Smothered me with love and hugs,
The kind that melts you instantly.
Ofcourse, my heart thumped
like a puppy dog,
Waiting to be let out!

I stuffed my pockets greedily
With loads of candid moments
A sweetness overload
that would last me a life time!
Excitement rippled through the room
as friends hugged
And squealed in delight
And danced into the night to
The heady refrain of familiar songs!
We sung it again and again
Like a cassette tape on rewind
The silly ones with catchy tunes
We loved to groove to
When we were still young.

Healing flowed from the hearts
Dripping with love and light.
A magic potion
For the weary souls longing
For some comic relief!
We huddled in the room like
Twittering Birds in twilight,
making quite a stir,

settling in for the night,

In the branches of a

Sprawling tree;

Excited to meet and whine

About the day that was,

The longest one before we

Start all over again,

In thunder lightning or crashing rain!

Home Coming

The table is laid out for me

And my soul quivers,

When my senses savour

The finest of flavors,

The best on offer.

I crave wistfully

For another slice

Of infinite goodness,

Another serving of glistening

Curried goodness

With dollops of love,

And sprinkles of kindness,

With a hint of tartness

The kind fresh lemons render.

Oh the magic and the echoes of laughter around the table

Is heady.

Come home to feel this

Infinite goodness.

From the fondant of love

that's overflowing

And can't be bottled up!

HOPE

Frozen Hope

Her aching branches

They creak

under the weight

of all the fresh snow

That fell last night

And now for sure-

looks all

dressed up

Like a pretty bride in white.

But truth be told

Her twigs are gaunt and dry

Fearful of the slightest breeze,

That can snap them into two.

"Be still" whispers

the voice in the Wind

As she crouches

Bent in fear-

The night shall pass

And soon you will be
Springing right back
With emerald leaves
Budding,
And you 'll be
The rising hope,
For someone with blurry eyes,
scanning the horizon
Looking out
Just for you,
Hopeful to live -
maybe even for
Just another day.

Sadness

Sadness wells up

And overflows yet again

Tearing to soak everything.

The linen,the pillows

Her soul and her skin so pale

Drenched in despair.

Joy bubbled over

In the lucid story of their love

And could be literally sensed

For miles,

The faint notes of the finest tones

wafting from their home.

But the chords of grief

Are often overlaid in

The finest masterpiece

Of notes and tones that move

Anyone to tears

And is often the bridge
Carrying the saddest heart across
The rugged hill.
The soul plummets just one more time
The earth seems to give away
When the hand that held you longest
Gently pulls away.
In that stark moment, you are
Cold and clammy and so lonely
Where fear and pain forage,
And sadness grips your soul.
It's the darkest night perhaps…
That you stayed up in years
soaked in tears,
Seeing your beloved's twinkling eyes
In every star, you gaze
Through your misty eyes.
There is no note or syllable
That can define your pain…
In the eye of this storm,
Strains of love
will reach your heart,
That's wells up in pride.

It shall not be broken but
The repairer of the breach
Is near.
He will not tarry,
He is the surgeon
And the shepherd of your soul.
Your beloved is,
imprinted in your heart.
His DNA is forever stamped,
In the recess of your heart.
In the overwhelming silence
You will savour peace.
The light will seep through the
Slatted window blinds,
To reach you like he would
To ruffle your hair,
And say ... Heyy...
And lean upon your heart.

Grief

Moments and memories,

Stoke a fire in my heart,

That keep me warm

On cold chilly nights.

But for now,

I want to be still

And I shut my eyes,

Like curtains pinched tight.

To keep out the light.

At least for some time...

I need to curl up,

In my Hiding Place

To be still and unseen;

To heal as I sleep

Drowning anxious thoughts

drumming in my head.

Silence shrouds me

And enshrines my soul
In times to come,
I will perhaps rise
from the ashes,
Like a painting restored
And sing like a phoenix.

Kintsugi – Beauty in Brokenness

Smashed.

Shattered it lay

A messy pile -

A mound of broken pottery...

Time nor wine

could not fix

Or bring back to life

This beautiful piece.

Broken shards

Lie everywhere.

Muffled sobs

Pierced the nights.

But Love.

Dabbed the wound,

And sealed the cracks,

With smelted gold,

Rivulets of gold,

Running down her back.

The story of the exquisite one

Had only just begun.

I am healed,

For I am strongest

In my broken place.

Wailing Walls

In panic people jostle
Impatiently and rush
Through dimly lit streets
Snaking through
Grimy residential spaces.
Washed out fascades
And tear-stained faces,
With resigned expressions
slip in and out,
Through the endless madness
Terrified as they return home
Hoping for a better day.
Miles away from alluring beaches
Full of people
With smiling faces
Is the moldy grey
Crumbly silhouette

Of a settlement

Now languishing in pain.

Caught in a time warp

The smoldering wails

of terrified children

Pierce the still night air.

Little do the perpetrators of fear

Hear the cries of the broken hearted.

Hard-hearted, their senses dullened,

They drown out the distant wails

From the city torn to shreds.

The River

Somewhere
Beyond the blues,
Majestic mountains
Give birth to
A rivulet so rare.
She trickled
Down the gorges,
Through the thicket
And the pebbles
she flowed.
Gurgling as she rushed,
Splashing and frothing,
Frolicking over the rocks.
Folks loved her,
They sat down beside her.
She flowed on,
Slowing for none.
Now and then,

Her temper rose,

And swept people off

With an angry roar

She cleared crazy curves...

Then one day,

The River met the Ocean,

And swirled in

a trance-like state,

Lost in the moment

Swelling up in pride

No roaring to be heard,

As deep meets the deep,

Resting peacefully as

She finds her destiny.

Hope

In the stormiest times

With no respite in sight

on a wintry night,

She huddled and nestled

cold and drenched

But firmly perched

on a rickety twig of

Hope.

Even when winds billowed

And the bough nearly broke

She remained unruffled.

Quiet as a mouse,

Not a squeak not a song

Until the crack of dawn.

In time, the storm receded

And through the canopy of green

A sliver of sun

Caught her eye.

Stronger and braver,

She crooned in joy,

with her chirping buddies

Cooing a

new song in delight!

Soul Story of an Alabaster Jar

Bottled and Shelved
For a long time to come
Was a rare perfume
In an Alabaster Jar.

The finest essence,
of, Life and Love,
Was poured into
the alabaster jar.

Sturdy and tall
Quite colorful and all
Unobserved in a corner,
Stood that tall Alabaster Jar.

An unwelcome tremor
From distant guns,
Shook that land one day;
and ungainly brought the
Alabaster down.

In that war zone
Now the Alabaster lay.
shattered to pieces
Among the dead.

The lingering scent
of love divine,
Wafts from
the alabaster jar.

The calming scent
Poured out became
The balm of Gilead
From a shattered Alabaster jar.

Through it All

On Windy days,
Whistling winds
Rustle through the leaves
Of the ancient oak
Standing tall.
When dark clouds rumble,
And pelting rains froth and fret
And pound the earth,
My favorite oak
Stands firm and tall.
Unruffled by the tempest,
ominous clouds,
grubby giants,
and fake friends that mushroom
On the ground,
The oak bares it all
Unmoved.

Bring it on she seems to thunder
Sweat grime and all.
I have seen and will see again
The goodness of God
Through it all.

Roads Less Travelled

I went many moons ago
On a journey
Down winding roads
That quickly got so narrow
Far sooner than I thought.

On those tricky trails
with twists and turns
And in the twilight hour
It's God s presence
That kept me sane-
On snaking treacherous trails.

Some desert roads
With thorns and thistles
And the scorching sun to add
Parched my throat
And burned to a crisp
all pretty plans I had!

Unchartered roads
Made me wince at times, fearful
of the perilous path ahead;
But that eased with encouraging friends
I met along the way.
blessed are the broken roads,
that took me through tough terrain.
even through torrential rains
Soaked & drenched,
In the end
I found my way to a safe haven
following broken roads.

Broken Chains

When
Threatening clouds
Cast an eerie shadow
For miles,
And
Uncertain days
tightened their grip,
As nightmares mercilessly
Trampled on her pretty dreams.,
Rain lashed on endlessly
Leaking from a stormy sky
That smacked of gloom
And bitter days.
When everyone was petrified,
She chose to savour
The sweet scent of summer rain
And fragments of sunshine that
Came her way.

She braided the bits, fragments and all
And with folded hands she prayed on
And trusted her God
To hold her steady through the storm
As she built her ark, her boat,her life
And took the moment in her stride,
and bit by bit,
she saw before her eyes,
A storm that came to harpoon her,
Now unarmed and limp,
Lies like tattered ropes at her feet.

FAITH

Hemmed in Love & Light

Walking through desolate places,
High-strung and parched,
Every twig that cracked
Sent shivers down my spine.

I spent wakeful hours
Groaning in pain, asking ...How? When?
I do not know if I took a wrong turn perhaps?
I had to plan an escape...

Love, with a gentle nudge,
And a tender hug snaps me back
Strips me of the barbs and thorns,
That nearly takes my breath away.

Today I am forever grateful,
For the light that leads me out
Of those frightful spaces,
I felt trapped in.

The piercing light through the cracks
Guides me out, of tunnels and turrets
I find myself and chart my path
Before another draft a plan,

Before I fall into yet another trap.
Love and light will find me out
Yank me by my soul
And mysteriously I will ride
Crests of giant waves, 'neath crimson skies
To usher in yet another day
Hemmed in Love and light.

The Potter

Dipping his hands in
Gooey clay
He swirls it with hopes
Of making a thing of beauty.

The hands that flung
The stars in the sky
Shapes me too
In an incredible way!

Like the glazed pottery reflects the awe
Of the happy traveller who pauses...
Longing to run their fingers
Over that perfectly sculpted curve.

Glistening in the sun, the sun-kissed Jade

and turquoise glaze

Reflects a work so precious!

I hear a gentle whisper

Rumblings in my soul like a distant thunder

You are exquisite, You are mine

I am your Potter

And You my clay.

Scarred Hands

Scarred and rugged are her hands,
Cupped in prayer folded to hold
That little light, she cups in the hollow
Of her praying hands.
The soft hands once fondled her baby,
And rocked the cradle,
now wrinkled and callused with time
Working night and day...
she cups that light in her child
To glow and connect, till the flame is strong
To keep others warm, in times to come.

Million Fireflies

Your smile and touch, like a million fireflies
Light up the night sky, on some of my darkest nights.
Tongues of fire descend, like a cleansing flame
To lick the smouldering embers,
That fans a revolution igniting my soul.

My wilting soul, bruised but not broken
Drained, emotional, hungover and scattered,
Is aglow and restored again,
With a million fireflies sent across my way
Swirling around, lighting up, my darkest nights.

King and I

In scorching heat and blinding blizzards
On the verge of defeat, when hope is bleak
And my vision so myopic
A gentle rush of wind just in time
Soothes my ruffled frame
And covers my shame and pain.

In the shifting shadows and twilight
I see, footprints in the sand
Of the One who carried me
Through the deafening roar of the waves
That dared not engulf me
Simply because He gently covers me unconditionally.

The gentle drumming raindrops
On my window and the gentle breeze
In the stillness of the night,
I sense the presence of my King.

So I hum through the night a song of gladness
In the valley and towering mountains alike
Tinged with hope, I gasp to see
My cup running over - with joy!

Lighthouse

The rumbling notes of distant thunder
And a hint of earthy scents
Sets my teeth on edge
Anxious thoughts, that crowd my brain
Ominously billow in, to cloud my mind
Breaking into a deluge of doubt
Recalling the day
When rain-soaked and cold
Anxious and troubled
I scampered for shelter.
Baring my fear-soaked heart
I wring out the last dregs of fear
Like fangs, they dig deep into my flesh

I prayed that my heart be held
My spirit calmed, in the storm
Now I am safe and still
Perched on a Rock.

The heart of God, a wellspring of strength

A lighthouse to the battered, reached out to me

When lost in the storm, longing to get home.

Snuggled in there,

in the heart of God

I stay... perched in comfort

My anxiety is at bay.

Easter

Straddled with baggage,

in the hollow of her heart

With fear stricken eyes she collapsed...

Tired, she dragged herself

Across several miles,

with no hope in sight

Stranded and homeless,

in an alien world.

Squinting she scanned,

the unending horizon

Not giving up.

She had heard of the Nazarene,

the gentle redeemer

Whose piercing gaze,

is all what it takes

To release the taut soul,

sickness and all.

Parched she walked to the well she noticed

Cupping her hands,

scooping cool water

Splashing her tear-stained face,

she felt His gaze

Turning around,

she fell to her knees

"Rabbi "she cried, He had found her.

Dear God

Dear God,
You came into my life
Or did I?
With a disruptive kind of love
That breaks barriers, and bring in rain,
Rain clouds pregnant with showers of blessing
Soaked me through and through
Your love is forged in me,
like a burning ember
Etches an intricate tattoo.
The scars of love,
swirling patterns of whorls
Geometric and abstract,
runs through and through
Filling every crevice, sealing and healing
Every snag and stitch in time.

Dear God,

How I can't wait to

tell another one -

I have risen from the ashes

And will sing to the end of time!

My World

In my world of sifting sands

A kaleidoscope, of brokenness

You are my friend

That holds my hand

When the heat and dust

Overwhelms my baby heart,

You hold me up, like no other has.

Endless love and endless grace lifts me up.

I cry and rest on your strong shoulder

And in a while when, my pain is all washed away

I sing

It is well with my soul, I am not forgotten, I am loved!!

Christmas To Me

Born in a stable, the lowliest one
Among the cattle, in a manger
With bales of hay where cattle are fed He lay.
He knocked on my door, one glorious morn
Came to my hearth, flooded my life
Such disruptive and unconditional love
Of another kind, that swept me off my feet
Only when I let Him in.

The train of his robe trails through the temple...
My heart - the temple – Where He reigns.

LEGACY

At Fifty

At fifty I am
Doing fun things authentically
As I pour out my heart
Embracing life!
Turning a deaf ear
To "what-ifs" and "why-not's".
Snuffing out shadows
That swallow up dreams.
I move on
And choose to drown out
The voice of naysayers
And deftly duck the blow
That could have smashed
My pretty nose!

Fifty and counting

The blessings pour in,

I steal a moment'

To gaze into the skies

Reverently.

Having crossed the 't's'and dotted the 'i's

As best as i could

I play heads n shoulders

knees n toes to another happy tune

Just to remember

Where I put my wallet keys and phone

Laughing as I do

I quietly slip into the shadows.

Rainbows and Roses

Aiming for the glistening arc,

Reaching for the stars,

I took off in a hurry,

When pretty young.

Dusting off the pixie dust,

I landed with a thud-

Not on a bed of roses

But on dusty tarmac!

I hit the road running,

Chasing wild dreams.

My escapades took me

Through scorching deserts,

And a few fancy landscapes,

Crossing moors and mountains

Thickets and tough terrain,

Tasting tangy flavors

Of several distant lands.

Bronzed skin and fine lines,

Few cuts and knees that hurt,

Marks this wizened soul,

Teaching me to

Slow down a bit to linger

And savor precious moments

Drenched in amazing flavors

That satiate my soul,

While chasing rainbows and roses!

Footprints by the Sea

The first tiny timid steps that
The baby took,
running to her mom
Were adorably wobbly
and got imprinted on mamma's heart!
Beaming and proud,mamma
Knelt beside her baby boo,
Who certainly learned a thing or two
About standing on her feet!
Mama wished the rising tide wouldn't wash away
Her baby's footprints but she sighed
In gratitude just the same,
Because she knew,
the frothy sea would soon
Kiss the shoreline
Wiping it all away.

All grown up now

The young woman

Takes a stroll by the sea,

Stronger and bolder

Digging deep to get a grip

Against the rising tide

Watching the swirling waves

on her olive skin

She ponders about

all the choices she took in life

That shaped her as she willed,

Hoping against hope that

Her footprints would be

The guiding lamp for her children.

Yet as she walks along the seafront

Strange as it may seem

When she looks over her shoulder

She sees all her footprints

Were wiped away by giant waves.

She stood there watching the ebbing tide

Wash away her footprints;

She plods with an awkward gait

As rushing foamy water

Swirls and tugs at her toes

She pauses and memories rush in

About crashing waves,

That she rode victoriously,

But often they were

A whiplash that shaped and moulded her,

Yet no legacy does she leave.

Imprinted in the sands of time

For her footprints on the seashore

Are washed away with time.

All that I Own

This is my story.
All that I own.
Walk if you must
For a mile with me
And I will tell you my story
It is all that I own.
And I 'll listen to yours
That which you own!

Silver and gold have I none
But a tapestry spun
Of love and a home.
The blaring din of traffic
And glaring city lights
At times, dim the light
Of the stories of lives
That is often unheard.
Sweet stories of valor

That needs to be heard,

Seep through the cracks

In the beams and broken walls.

I linger long enough

To listen and learn from

Stories soaked in

Endurance and hope.

And I catch a glimpse of heaven

Entangled in the threads of humanity

I pause to listen

And in the stillness of the night

I hear -

Muffled sobs, a gasp,

A sigh of hope,

All caught in the warp of time.

This is their story, entangled in mine

That's more precious than silver or gold.

Who Walks in Beauty?

She is no longer
Apologetic
Insecure or invisible
But I would add
Invincible is she!
she is a fine fragrance
That nudges hidden memories
Out from the attic of my brain.

Body shamed and groomed
Nudged and cajoled,
To whiten and lighten
Her skin to a point it was
Like translucent tumblers,
Glistening and bronzed.
With hair that was scorched
And colored and treated
That drain and strain.
Perennial pretensions

Weighing down hearts
And wallets.
Constantly she battled
Defects and norms.
These are perhaps
Perpetuated notions
That strips so many
Of dignity and confidence?

Crossing the fifties
Rough seas and seasons
I grin at the equator
Triumphantly!
Not a feminist or feline
But feminine for sure
Loving my wrinkles
Curls and grey hair
Stretch marks and all!
An unfiltered unedited
Unapologetic creature
With splotches and blotches,
But grateful and graceful,
She walks tall and in truth
She walks in beauty.

Wispy Greys

Wispy grey curls-
her crowning glory
Speak of
Windswept days...
A few that spluttered
And wheezed

And refused to budge,
And few that steam rolled
And took her across the oceans!
Through it all
Her flouncy hair
Like a flag unfurled,
Dancing in the wind
whips across
Her salty skin,
Shouting out to all
The world
About a life well lived!

Fine lines on her forehead,
Crinkly skin around
Her sparkling eyes,
Fine silvery hair that
Plays peekaboo and
Whisper
Of wisdom and grace,
Shines through
Like a dancing moonbeam
On a pitch-dark night.

No More Labels

All my life I darted,

Between shadows and my fears,

And nearly drowned in an endless sea of dreams,

Rowing a run-down boat riddled with holes.

I wondered why I was

in that borrowed boat.

I was a runner

Running from pain and shame

With often a confetti of

Sticky post-it notes with

With labels that I hated.

stuck to my heel.

She is this and she is that

I heard voices in my head

Will the gossip and the haters

Wear my worn-out shoes

And bear the bunion's pain
The shame and all the burden
That's mine alone to bear?

No one can rewrite my story
Or sign off with their name
Against the story that's surging up
To water several hearts
That need to hear it
To usher in the green!
Stories like mine
Bookmarked and shelved,
Often bear the mark of pain
But births a generation
The testament of truth.
It took me time to learn
Not to be a clone of someone else.
Authentic is my name
I am the salt you find in the sea
And the tears that soak your pillow
I could never change to be
The sugar in the teapot
That can never be me.

Our Home and Hearth

Like faded grass

In the sun scorched fields

Another year just wilts away!

And sheaves of memories

Like bales of hay

Are bundled tight

For times ahead.

Together we huddle

Through laughter and tears,

And wintry nights,

Weaving memories as we walk

The talk

Mirroring godly insight

We build our home,

Unshaken by

Whipping winds or pounding waves.

I stand unfazed by trouble n snares

That come knocking at times,

As each day will by and by

Like wilting grass

And the fading flowers

Wither away with time.

Because we build upon

Hope n faith, the solid rock

On which we stand

Powered by a sturdy heart

That beats on and on

And beckons you too my friend

To come home to dine with us

To rest your tired mind!

Rich in Love

I am the richest one
Lemme tell u why
Cos' i own my day
With the maze and the haze
The traps the pits,
The highs and lows,
The sweat and grime and stilettos!
Content with a whiff of love
(and the coffee
Brewing on my stove,)
And of course
piquant food
That I whip up and dig in too!
And then of course
There is my pet who needs a walk
And he makes me stretch and run!
When trouble brews
I try not to let it

Sear or burn my hand and heart -
And try of course to not pout
And ruin what is left
Of a precious day
Filled with umpteen possibilities
That constantly comes my way...
Sunshine and balmy breeze
And the rain that pings
My skin,
Remind me to relish
My cup of hot coffee
And affirm once again that
I am the richest girl today...
Cos' I own my day and wear it too
Like a crown on my brow,
And plan to be just the same
Again and again.

Pearls of Wisdom

Wear me if you want
On your beating heart
Or like a dangling tassel
On your silk scarf
I wouldn't make a noise
To be heard.
Vanity is beyond me
And not my cup of tea!

What's in your clasp
Is of more worth than
All the desolate cities
Built by human hands.
So hold me gently
In the cusp of your heart
And reverently in your grasp
And may pearls of wisdom
Be the tassels on your scarf!

Knit

Some folks knit,

With needles.

I with words.

Lift and toss and

Twirl thoughts and ideas

Loop and neatly knot

It tight.

Repeat and move on.

The patterns and weaves

Speak about endless sunsets

And second chances.

With a sigh of relief

I knit.

Disentangle knots with ease

Grateful for innocuous boring days

When nothing earthshaking

Happened.

But I continue to knit,

In quietude

drowning out the noise;

Hopeful instead to be the voice

Of reason,

To bring together salty hearts

And communities.

To help heal and darn

Broken breaches and trenches

With intricate patterns

That darn every snag.

I feel the rush of love and life

And the healing hug of the Divine

As I continue to knit.